TECHN
FOR BU
PEOPLE

M000303931

BCS, THE CHARTERED INSTITUTE FOR IT

BCS, The Chartered Institute for IT, champions the global IT profession and the interests of individuals engaged in that profession for the benefit of all. We promote wider social and economic progress through the advancement of information technology science and practice. We bring together industry, academics, practitioners and government to share knowledge, promote new thinking, inform the design of new curricula, shape public policy and inform the public.

Our vision is to be a world-class organisation for IT. Our 70,000-strong membership includes practitioners, businesses, academics and students in the UK and internationally. We deliver a range of professional development tools for practitioners and employees. A leading IT qualification body, we offer a range of widely recognised qualifications.

Further Information
BCS, The Chartered Institute for IT,
First Floor, Block D,
North Star House, North Star Avenue,
Swindon, SN2 1FA, United Kingdom.
T +44 (0) 1793 417 424
F +44 (0) 1793 417 444
www.bcs.org/contact

http://shop.bcs.org/

TECHNICAL WRITING FOR BUSINESS PEOPLE

Carrie Marshall

bcs
The Chartered Institute for IT

Printed by Amazon POD

BCS and the BCS logo are the registered trade marks of the British Computer Society, charity number 292786 (BCS).

Published by BCS Learning & Development Ltd, a wholly owned subsidiary of BCS, The Chartered Institute for IT, First Floor, Block D, North Star House, North Star Avenue, Swindon, SN2 1FA, UK.
www.bcs.org

Paperback ISBN: 978-1-78017-4464
PDF ISBN: 978-1-78017-4471
ePUB ISBN: 978-1-78017-4488
Kindle ISBN: 978-1-78017-4495

British Cataloguing in Publication Data.
A CIP catalogue record for this book is available at the British Library.

Disclaimer:
The views expressed in this book are of the author(s) and do not necessarily reflect the views of the Institute or BCS Learning & Development Ltd except where explicitly stated as such. Although every care has been taken by the authors and BCS Learning & Development Ltd in the preparation of the publication, no warranty is given by the authors or BCS Learning & Development Ltd as publisher as to the accuracy or completeness of the information contained within it and neither the authors nor BCS Learning & Development Ltd shall be responsible or liable for any loss or damage whatsoever arising by virtue of such information or any instructions or advice contained within this publication or by any of the aforementioned.

Publisher's acknowledgements
Reviewers: Oliver Lindberg and Cliff Hobbs
Publisher: Ian Borthwick
Commissioning Editor: Rebecca Youé
Production Manager: Florence Leroy
Project Manager: Sunrise Setting Ltd
Cover work: Alex Wright
Picture credits: DenisProduction.com / Shutterstock
Typeset by Lapiz Digital Services, Chennai, India.

CONTENTS

LIST OF FIGURES

AUTHOR

Carrie Marshall is a journalist, copywriter, ghostwriter and broadcaster from Glasgow. A professional writer for 20 years, she has written thousands of features, columns, reviews and news stories for a huge range of magazines, newspapers, websites and trade publications. As a copywriter she has crafted copy for some of the biggest names in the technology, retail, audio and finance industries, and as a novelist she sold enough copies of her self-published debut to buy a car. Not a great car, but still: a car! Under various names Carrie has written 11 non-fiction books, co-written six more and co-wrote a six-part Radio 2 documentary series. She blogs at bigmouthstrikesagain.com and tweets as @carrieinglasgow.

PREFACE

Technical writing is so important that in a better world, the people who do it would all sit on solid gold thrones being fed grapes by their grateful colleagues.

I'm only half joking. Technical writing is what saves companies from terrible mistakes and operational inefficiencies, from irate employees and confused customers. And it's something we only tend to notice when it goes wrong.

One of my favourite examples of that involved a spaceship. The full story is in Chapter 12, but the short version is that a simple technical writing error meant that the two teams making a $125 million Mars orbiter for the National Aeronautics and Space Administration (NASA) used different measurements. Nobody spotted the mistake until the probe messed up its atmospheric burn and headed straight for the sun.

Most technical writing isn't that dramatic, but it can still make an incredible difference to a business. It can make the rollout of a new information technology (IT) system so much smoother. It can make trainers' lives better and their training more useful. It can translate the most complex concepts and express them in the best way for any audience.

Technical writing gets the right information to the right people in the right way. And this book explains how to do that – not just in printed material but in online text and multimedia too.

In **Chapter 1** I'll explain what technical writing is and why the most important tool isn't a really good pen or keyboard.

In **Chapter 2** we'll step through the key stages of technical writing from setting the specification to revision and archiving. We'll also discuss the importance of separating style from content.

If you don't know who you're writing for, you shouldn't start writing yet. **Chapter 3** explains why.

Chapter 4 shows you how to break down even the most forbidding project into bite-size chunks, and why that's good for you and for your readers.

Chapter 5 looks at the dangers of assuming things, such as readers' expertise or knowledge.

In **Chapter 6** we'll look at the importance of precision and the best ways to vanquish vagueness.

I love humour, but as we'll discover in **Chapter 7**, it's best avoided in technical documents.

In **Chapter 8** we'll take inspiration from coding and optimise our text to do more with less.

Chapter 9 shows how weak and woolly writing can make even the best content boring.

In **Chapter 10** we'll look at visual ways to present information and break up large blocks of text.

In **Chapter 11** we'll identify the ways in which editing can make good writing great, and the traps technical writers sometimes fall into.

And in **Chapter 12** we'll explore the technical writing house of horrors: the commas, letters and basic errors that have destroyed spaceships and historic businesses alike.

Let's get to work.

1 WHAT IS TECHNICAL WRITING?

Technical writing is about communicating key information to the people who need it in the most suitable way and format. That might be printed material, but it could also be a graphic or a video.

That information might be a tutorial for a software application, a guide to using heavy machinery safely, a diagnostic aide for medical practitioners or a guidance note about new legislation.

If you work in a technical or specialist field of any kind you may be a technical writer already.

According to the Society for Technical Communications, technical communication has one or more of the following characteristics:[1]

1. Communicating about technical or specialised topics, such as computer applications, medical procedures or environmental regulations.
2. Communicating through printed documents or technology, such as web pages, help files or social media sites.
3. Providing instructions about how to do something, regardless of the task's technical nature.

According to the Institute of Scientific and Technical Communicators:[2]

---

[1] Society for Technical Communications (n.d.) *Defining technical communication.* Available from www.stc.org/about-stc/defining-technical-communication/
[2] Institute of Scientific and Technical Communicators (n.d.) *Why do we need technical communication?* Available from www.istc.org.uk/value-of-technical-communication/why-do-we-need-technical-communication/

Technical communication tends to answer the six important questions. These are: what, when, why, where, who and how – and often with an emphasis on the 'how'. It may be provided as text, images, video, simulations, online help or in a number of other formats. The information in technical communication is targeted to the needs of the people using it to complete a task.

Technical writers are often translators. We take things that others may find complex or intimidating and simplify them, making them clear and user friendly.

Your organisation will benefit from effective technical writing. Effective technical writing clears up confusion, and helps people to understand crucial concepts, new systems and important procedures. A help document that isn't helpful or training materials that don't help the trainer cost money, both in terms of time spent and customer or employee satisfaction. The technical writer enables the business to communicate more efficiently and more effectively – and if they encounter particular issues that cause particular problems, they can be the early warning of issues the business really needs to fix.

Technical writing is often thought of as the creation of help files and user manuals, and it does include those things. But it may also mean creating reports about technical or scientific issues, or writing safety guidance on how to operate potentially dangerous products, or designing a flow chart on how to troubleshoot an electric car, or creating the datasheet for a smartphone.

Here's an example from Apple, explaining what to do with a device that has frozen.[3]

On an iPhone X, iPhone 8, or iPhone 8 Plus: Press and quickly release the Volume Up button. Press and quickly release the Volume Down button. Then, press and hold the Side button until you see the Apple logo.

This is from the specification sheet for the Samsung Galaxy S8 phone, explaining the options for playing its video on a TV.[4]

---

[3] From this page: https://support.apple.com/en-gb/ht201412
[4] From this page: www.samsung.com/global/galaxy/galaxy-s8/specs/

Wireless: Smart View (Miracast 1080p at 30 fps, mirroring support available for devices supporting Miracast or Google Cast.)

With cable: supports DisplayPort over USB type-C. Supports video out when connecting via HDMI Adapter. (DisplayPort 4K 60 fps)

And this is an example from barbecue firm Weber on how to cook safely.[5]

Oil should only be used if absolutely necessary and applied to the cooking grate using kitchen roll.

Although I'll talk about technical writing throughout this book, technical writing in the 21st century usually means more than just writing. The job of a technical writer is to help people with the things they need to know, and to use whatever tools enable them to do that best – and today, that toolkit contains all kinds of media and apps.

THE TECHNICAL WRITER'S TOOLKIT

The days when all technical writing was printed paragraphs or lists on paper are long gone. While printed text is still important, it's become part of a toolkit that embraces a variety of content and delivery methods, including:

- **Audio and video.** Such media may involve a range of techniques and content: a video might be narrated over footage of the task being described, or could be scripted to deliver a promotional message. The content may be delivered from a streaming site such as YouTube, from the organisation's own website or via a smartphone or tablet app.

- **Online knowledge bases and chatbots.** A knowledge base is a fancy name for a help system: they are

---

[5] From this page: www.weber.com/GB/en/top-bbq-tips/safety/gafc3.html

databases of information, usually presented in the form of short articles, that you can search for specific words, phrases or topics. Chatbots are an evolution of knowledge bases. Instead of users searching for the solution to a problem and wading through pages of results, chatbots are automated apps that deliver human-style interaction to help people get the information they need.

- **Content management systems (CMSs).** CMSs are apps, often web-based, that are designed to collate, manage and publish a wide range of content. One of the most famous CMSs is the online publishing platform Wordpress, which is used for small blogs and giant media sites alike.

- **Social media.** From Twitter tweets to lengthy articles on LinkedIn or Medium.

- **Downloadable documents.** Often in Word or PDF format.

As you'll discover in later chapters, different media require different approaches and different kinds of writing.

THE MOST IMPORTANT THING YOU NEED AS A TECHNICAL WRITER (AND NO, IT ISN'T A REALLY GOOD PEN)

The most important thing you need isn't talent, a way with words or a whizzy word processing app. They all help, but the most important thing is time.

Technical writing is a craft, not an art, and the more time you spend doing it, the better you become. If you have time to learn the ins and outs of the subject (or to interview the people who do), time to plan, time to create the appropriate documents and time to fine-tune, edit, assess and test them, then you should find that you create technical writing that does its job very well.

That doesn't mean you won't benefit from some expert advice though. There are traps you don't want to fall into, bad habits you don't want to adopt and lots of killer tips and tricks that can make your writing even better. And they all just happen to be in this book.

KEY TAKEAWAYS

- Technical writing communicates key information to the people who need it.
- It communicates that information in the most effective way.
- The most important thing you need for good technical writing is time.

2 SEVEN STEPS TO HEAVEN: THE TECHNICAL WRITING CYCLE

There may have been three steps to heaven for Eddie Cochran,[6] but for a technical writer there are seven. The process of creating and publishing technical writing can be broken down into these seven parts:

1. identify the specification, audience and scope;
2. planning;
3. research and writing;
4. testing, reviewing and revision;
5. delivery;
6. evaluation and feedback;
7. revision, archiving or destruction.

Let's explore each section in turn. We'll also look at a few general considerations for a technical writing project too.

1. SPECIFICATION, AUDIENCE AND SCOPE

The first part of any technical writing project is to identify the who, the what and the why. Who are you writing for? What information do they need? Why and where do they need it? These pieces of information are crucial. If you don't know who you're writing for, you can't know how best to communicate, what level of knowledge or expertise you can expect them to have or what the best medium for communicating with them

---

[6] One, find a girl you love; two, she falls in love with you; three, you kiss and hold her tightly. 'Three Steps to Heaven', May 1960.

would be. An airplane safety card isn't much use if it's in a language the passenger doesn't understand.

2. PLANNING

Good technical writing takes time. Once you've identified the who, what and why, you need to plan out the how, the where and the when. How should this information be delivered? What resources do you need in order to do it properly? What is the best medium for the message you're communicating and how should the message be structured? When does it need to be delivered? How is it going to be tested and reviewed?

3. RESEARCH AND WRITING

For many of us this is the easy, fun bit. It's described very well in the parable of the engineer and the hammer.[7] If you don't know it, it goes something like this.

One day, a factory's most important machine breaks down at the worst possible time. Already losing money at a frightening rate and unable to get the machine going again, the company has no choice but to call in a very experienced and very expensive engineer. He strolls in, pulls out a hammer and whacks the machine very hard, just once. The machine immediately bursts into life and the engineer hands the manager an invoice for £10,000.

The manager is outraged. Ten grand for hitting a machine once? That's daylight robbery! He demands the engineer account for the charge and demands an itemised invoice with a full breakdown of the engineer's fees.

---

[7] Credited to multiple authors; according to QI (https://quoteinvestigator.com/2017/03/06/tap/), the earliest recorded instance was in *The Journal of the Society of Estate Clerks of Works* of Winchester, England in 1908. See https://books.google.co.uk/books?id=w-nVAAAAIAAJ&q=%22tap-tap

The engineer agrees. The following day, a new invoice arrives and this time it's itemised.

Hammer: £5;

Knowing the right place to hit with a hammer: £9,995.

This part of the technical writing process is your £5 hammer because with a good specification, the right resources and a solid plan you're just typing here. The real value comes from what you do before and after you actually write, and from the knowledge and experience you bring to the project.

4. TESTING, REVIEWING AND REVISION

This section is as important as the actual research and writing. It's when you discover what other people do with your documents, and it's often an eye-opener: if you've assumed too little or too much knowledge on your readers' part that will soon become glaringly obvious, as will any major omissions or mistakes. It's really important to put your ego aside during this part of the process as your goal is to create the best possible end product with the resources, time and budget available to you. Criticism and highlighting errors helps you achieve that.

5. DELIVERY

Delivering the finished product isn't the end; it's the end of the beginning. It's a good time to give yourself a pat on the back for a job well done, but it's a job you'll normally return to.

6. EVALUATION AND FEEDBACK

Issues or problems with technical writing don't always appear during the testing and revision stage. Sometimes the writing needs to be used in real-world situations in order for any flaws to become apparent. And that's okay, because you've already thought about that and ensured that your readers can and will provide feedback in a form that you can use to refine the job, solve any problems and polish it to perfection. This is also the stage where localisation would take place if necessary; for example, if your material needs to be rewritten for another language, market or audience.

7. REVISION, ARCHIVING OR DESTRUCTION

Many technical documents have a limited lifespan: hardware, software or systems change; legislation is repealed or reformed; mission creep may mean that a particular system's role becomes much wider than initially imagined. That means documentation needs to be under constant review: updated where appropriate, retired when no longer necessary, destroyed if it contains secrets that shouldn't be revealed.

In this book our focus will be on the research and writing stage: the knowing which bit to hit with our hammer.

TECHNICAL WRITING IN A TEAM

Some technical writing jobs are too big for one person to do without help. If you're going to be writing as part of a technical writing team, it's crucial to have somebody in charge of the whole project. That person may well be you.

The person in charge of a technical writing team is effectively a project manager. Their job is to allocate different parts of the project to different people, to ensure that those parts are done correctly and on time, and to ensure consistency across the entire project. It's a job that begins at the very early planning stages and continues through publication and review.

A QUICK WORD ABOUT WRITING APPS

For a technical writing project, you don't need a dedicated writing app if you've got access to Microsoft Word, Apple

Pages, Google Docs, OpenOffice or other Office-style software, and, of course, you can write effectively with nothing more than a notepad and a Biro.

However, if you're going to be doing a lot of technical writing it's worth considering a writer-specific app such as Scrivener,[8] which is available for Windows, Mac and iOS. It isn't expensive – at the time of writing it's around £33 for computers and £20 for iOS devices – and it'll pay for itself many times over. It's particularly useful for large projects and for projects that will be published in multiple formats both in print and online.

In a team-based writing environment, your priorities may be slightly different: you can of course use whatever writing app you prefer, but when it comes to collaborating with others then you're making life unnecessarily difficult if you don't use a platform with instant, effortless collaboration and communication tools.

You're probably familiar with email tennis, when the same file or files are constantly moving backwards and forwards between relevant people who add their comments or changes. Staying on top of that can be very difficult, and it's easy to end up with people receiving documents that have since been updated or making comments that others have already made. A good online service such as Office 365, Google Docs or iCloud prevents that from happening by giving everybody the most up-to-date version of the document.

You might also find that your favourite writing app works with third party sharing and collaboration services, so, for example, if you use Scrivener, you can synchronise your documents with the cloud-based storage and synchronisation service Dropbox, so that people without Scrivener can open, edit and comment on them. Dropbox and its rivals also offer online collaboration tools that you can use without having to go through Scrivener first.

---

[8] See www.literatureandlatte.com/scrivener/overview

There are two key features you may need for online collaboration: commenting and change tracking. The former enables relevant parties to add notes to the text without actually changing it – suggestions or links to other things to include, perhaps, or questions about particular bits – and for you to respond or mark comments as resolved. And the second feature, change tracking, enables you to see exactly what changes others have made and to accept or reject those changes as appropriate.

Many apps enable you to set different levels of access for different people or groups, so you might give other members of your team full edit access but limit non-writers' access to commenting and highlighting only.

You don't necessarily need to be using the same apps to collaborate. Microsoft Office's commenting and change tracking works in some other apps, so a .docx file from Word should still include its comments and change tracking if you open it in Apple's Pages (and remember to export it in .docx format to preserve the tracking information).

A QUICK WORD ABOUT FORMATTING TEXT

When you're writing, it's a very good idea to use as little text formatting as possible. That's particularly true if you're going to be writing for multiple platforms, such as printed documentation and online systems such as CMSs: what looks good as a Word document may require extensive editing if you paste it into a CMS that uses different formatting options.

In the past I wrote everything and stored it as plain text (.txt) documents without any formatting whatsoever, but in recent years I've become a convert to Markdown.[9] Markdown is supported by a huge range of writing apps, and it's designed to make creating and reusing formatted text easy.

---

[9] See http://daringfireball.net/projects/markdown/ for an explanation of Markdown.

It does that with simple shortcuts, so, for example, if I want to format a bit of text as a heading, I put a single hash in front of it. Two hashes means heading 2, three means heading 3 and so on. Other shortcuts enable me to add bullet points or numbered lists, hyperlinks or blocks of code. The documents are all stored as plain text files, but Markdown-aware writing apps can export in a range of unformatted and formatted file types such as Microsoft Word, PDF, rich text format, ePub and so on. All you need to do is choose the format and template you want to use, and your writing app will create the appropriate file.

It's the same write-once run-anywhere approach you see in web design, where page content (the XHTML file) is separated from the formatting (the relevant style sheet); changing the style sheet (or the template, in my writing app), changes the formatting without having to go through the document and replacing every formatting option.

If you want to use Markdown you don't necessarily need to find a new writing app, although there are some very good ones out there – my favourite, the Mac/iOS app Ulysses,[10] has become my go-to app for all my writing tasks from notes to books. If you're using Microsoft Word on Windows, the Writage app[11] adds Markdown support to Word from versions 2010 onwards.

KEY TAKEAWAYS

- Writing is easy. The real work is in the preparation and revision.
- Testing, evaluation and feedback are crucial.
- Delivering the finished project isn't the end of the job.

---

[10] See https://ulyssesapp.com/
[11] See www.writage.com

Printed by Amazon POD

3   KNOW YOUR AUDIENCE

We touched on this in the previous chapter and it's absolutely crucial. You need the answers to these questions before you type a single character – Who are you writing for? What do they know already? What information do they need? Why do they need it? Where will they need it, and in what format?

Without that information, it's almost impossible to produce an effective piece of technical writing. Technical writing is usually the solution to a business need or problem. If you don't know what the need or problem is, how can you possibly solve it?

Let's start with the who.

WHO ARE YOU WRITING FOR?

Audiences fall into four main categories, although of course there's some overlap between them. They are:

- experts;
- technicians;
- management;
- end users or customers.

Experts are exactly who you think they are: they're the people who invented the product, designed the system or wrote the software. They're usually the people you talk to so that you can translate their expertise for the other less expert audiences.

Technicians are the people with technical knowledge and experience: they're the technical support technicians, the mechanics, the operators.

Management are the people who make the decisions about whether to buy, implement, retire or upgrade things. They often (but not always) have fairly limited technical knowledge.

End users or customers are the people being trained, being provided with information or being sold to. They usually (but again, not always) have less technical knowledge than the experts or technicians.

Each of these audiences will expect different kinds of information. Experts don't want background information because they know the subject inside out. End users don't want a barrage of technical data. Management often just want to know the bottom line.

It's possible to make the same content for all four kinds of audiences, but it's rarely desirable. Trying to please everybody often means pleasing nobody. That's because what each group knows and the information they expect can be very different.

PERSONAS IN TECHNICAL WRITING

Personas are ways of describing types of people based not just on who they are, but on what they need. For example, if you're writing a how-to guide for a word processing document, the needs of a university student will be different to the needs of someone who'll be bashing out letters. They both need to create documents, but the kinds of documents they need to create are very different and will therefore require different information.

Personas are particularly important in marketing communications, where you need to speak a different language or highlight different features for different types of audience, but they can be very useful in all kinds of technical writing: for example, the end users or customers described in the previous section will not be a homogenous mass. The customers of a technology product may range from cash-rich, enthusiastic, what-does-this-button-do early adopters to more cautious, conservative users who find the whole thing intimidating.

Some people may inhabit multiple personas, and documents may be structured in such a way that they can deliver for different personas simultaneously: for example, by providing a just-the-facts approach for the time poor and a separate section with more detail for the people who need it.

WHAT DO THEY ALREADY KNOW?

One of the things that helps inform our audience grouping is the audience characteristics. One of the most important such characteristics is background knowledge. That might be practical knowledge, theoretical knowledge or a mixture of both.

Let's say you're writing about a tablet computer. The experts don't need to know how to use one – they probably know how to make one from whatever's lying around. But somebody who's never seen a tablet before or never used one with that particular mobile operating system is going to need a lot more hand-holding.

Similarly, if you're writing about climate change, the information you present for climate scientists is going to be very different from the information you might put in a document aimed at interested members of the public.

These differences aren't a problem, but they can add complexity and cost to your project. The more diverse your audience in terms of expertise and knowledge, the more difficult it is to write for that wide audience. Examples and analogies that work really well for one group may be completely inappropriate for another. Terms that one group know intimately may require translation or explanation for other groups. Theory that's interesting to experts may bore everybody else silly.

There's also education and background to consider too. Our goal is clarity, and that means using the right language for our readers. Language that's just fine for somebody with a degree in Mechanical and Electrical Engineering and 20 years in high-tech fabrication may not be fine for someone who's fresh out of secondary school.

The big danger here is in assumed knowledge, which we'll cover in detail in Chapter 5. If you assume that your readers are all end users you may end up oversimplifying things, which will annoy the technicians and the experts. But if you assume too much knowledge, you'll make the end users and potential customers unhappy instead.

WHAT DO THEY NEED TO KNOW, AND WHY?

This is another thing that will differ from audience to audience. End users will generally need to know what to do to make X happen, or what to do if Y happens. Potential customers will want to know why they should buy this and not that. Management will want to know the financial implications of something and so on.

Once again, making the same document work for these different audiences adds complexity and cost. It's often better to produce separate documents for each distinct group. For example, you might produce a detailed document for decision makers but a punchy summary for end users.

That might involve using different delivery methods too. The online college FutureLearn does this very well: when you do a course such as Digital Skills: User Experience,[12] much of the content is delivered via video but the site also provides full transcripts you can refer to at your leisure for those segments

---

[12] See www.futurelearn.com/courses/digital-skills-user-experience

of the audience that prefer that – and, unlike the video, those transcripts are searchable on your Mac or PC. The transcripts are also accessible for people. Other online courses deliver material in different ways.

WHERE AND WHEN DO THEY NEED TO KNOW IT?

The answers to this question will help to inform your choice of medium. The reader may need the information to be presented to them in a searchable online help system, or as tooltips on a CMS. It may be a troubleshooting guide at the end of a detailed but fairly dull product manual. Or the information may need to be very visible and readable in the event of an emergency. You'll often need to use different strokes for different folks.

KEY TAKEAWAYS

- Don't start writing until you know exactly who you're writing for.
- Different audiences may require very different presentation styles and language.
- Writing for multiple audiences increases cost and complexity.

4 BREAK IT DOWN: THE IMPORTANCE OF A TASK-BASED APPROACH

There are many names for it – chunking, topic-based writing, task-based writing, modular writing and many more – but whatever you want to call it, one of the most effective ways to produce technical writing is to take the overall project and break it down into small parts.

There are two very good reasons for doing that. The first is that it makes it easier for the reader to find the information they need as quickly as possible, instead of wading through lots of information they don't need. Guidance that's hard to find is often guidance that doesn't get read.

And the second is that it makes the writing and editing process much easier too.

A task-based approach is particularly useful when you're creating writing for multiple platforms, or when your writing can be or will be reused in other projects.

Think of each section as a link in a chain, or a building block. You can add more links or blocks move them around or take out ones you decide you no longer need and the overall structure – the chain, or the building you made from your blocks – remains.

BREAK IT DOWN (BUT NOT TOO MUCH)

Breaking a project down into individual sections is a good idea, provided that everything still makes sense. If the sections are too small or don't seem to be connected to the ones before and after them, you can lose the flow of your document and make it harder for the reader to follow.

That's why I've gone for the term 'task-based' here. If you create your content with the reader in mind and always ask 'what is the reader trying to do here?' you can avoid creating something that isn't as helpful as it could be.

Let's take a simple example: the photos app on your phone, which is where every photo you take ends up.

If you were given the job of creating tutorials for that app, the task-based approach might produce a structure something like this:

- how to load the app, see your photos and move around;
- how to get rid of photos you don't want;
- how to organise photos by album, date, place or people;
- how to turn animated photos into still images;
- how to get a still image from a video clip;
- how to make your photos look better:
  - filters and effects;
  - cropping and rotating;
  - auto-enhance;
  - light and colour levels;
- how to send photos to others:
  - sending by email or SMS;
  - cloud photo sharing;
  - third party services such as Flickr or Dropbox;
- wireless photo printing.

When you've got that structure the tutorial pretty much writes itself. From a reader's point of view, it's easy to find the particular feature you need information about, and from a publishing point of view, it works well both in print and online.

Many writing apps enable you to use that structure for your document files too, so, for example, if you decided later that 'How to make your photos look better' should go at the very front it's just a matter of dragging that file to the top of the structure.

When you're creating task-based content it's a good idea to go through the task as you write about it, because that often helps you find opportunities to help the reader even more. For example, you might be writing about a machine part that isn't too easy to identify when the machine isn't spotlessly clean, so you could decide to include a diagram or photo. You might find that many users encounter a specific problem or error message at a certain point, so you could put in advice on what to do if that occurs. There might be a particular knack in getting a device to do what you want it to do. Or you might be describing something that has a range of possible settings, in which case you could provide a table of the appropriate options.

It's important to consider what's best for the reader rather than what's best for you, though – a document consisting entirely of tables can be rather forbidding.

This is a just-in-time approach to information delivery: rather than give the reader lots of information up-front and expect them to remember it, you give them exactly what they need exactly when they need it.

THE OTHER BIG BENEFIT OF A TASK-BASED APPROACH

If you're a project manager, a fan of life-hack websites or a user of the Getting Things Done productivity system[13] you'll know

---

[13] A very popular productivity system created by David Allen, https://gettingthingsdone.com

this one already: instead of trying to do an entire project, if you concentrate instead on smaller, more achievable chunks you'll find it much less intimidating and much easier to plan and manage. Writing the entire documentation for a new system sounds like the kind of job that'll take over your life. Writing a how-to on exporting data to Excel sounds like something you can do before your next tea break.

That's important because procrastination loves to whisper in writers' ears, telling them that the job is far too big to start today so they might as well leave it until tomorrow. And of course, tomorrow comes along and procrastination has reasons not to start then too. If like many people you're expected to fit your technical writing into a job that has many other pressing demands and responsibilities, putting things off can be very tempting – and ultimately disastrous, because there's always some more pressing matter demanding your attention and keeping you away from a job that's becoming more intimidating the longer you leave it. Breaking up your project into smaller tasks and making sure you put each task in the diary is a really good way of getting procrastination to shut up.

KEY TAKEAWAYS

- Task-based writing is easier to navigate, to organise and to create.
- Ask: 'what exactly is the reader trying to do or achieve here?' Breaking big projects into chunks makes them less intimidating.

5   ASSUME NOTHING

Assumptions are bad for technical writing. Just because you know something doesn't mean that the reader does.

If we write content based on the assumption that our reader knows something and our reader doesn't, then our content could be completely incomprehensible to them.

The big danger of assumptions is that if the reader doesn't know or doesn't fully understand what you're talking about, then the information you're trying to pass on won't be passed on.

MAKING ASSUMPTIONS

Here's a great example. If you show a photograph of a floppy disk to young people, many of them will think you're showing them a photo of a 3D-printed 'Save' icon. They're too young to have encountered floppies.

It's a funny story, and true. But I'm also making assumptions when I tell you it. I'm assuming that you're old enough to know what floppy disks were. I'm assuming that you called them floppies like I did. I'm assuming your idea of a floppy is the same as mine, the plastic 3.5" floppy disk and not its 5.25" or 8" predecessors. I'm assuming that you know what 3D printing is, and what the 'Save' icon looks like in Microsoft Windows and so on.

That's a lot of assumptions to hang a fun little story on.

I've deliberately taken my assumptions explanation too far, but I'm making a serious point. If you assume that your reader knows X, Y and Z, you may well be wrong – and if your writing is based on that assumption, then it may be of no value to the reader.

Writers tend to make incorrect assumptions about their readers' knowledge in one of two ways. One, they assume the reader knows more than they actually do, which can cause confusion or possibly even danger if you're assuming knowledge of safety-related issues they don't have. Or two, they underestimate their readers' knowledge and end up patronising them, which rarely makes the reader think good things about the author or the author's document.

Getting the balance right can be tricky. It's partly knowing your audience, which was described in Chapter 3, and it's partly testing and editing, which is when incorrect assumptions tend to become apparent.

You might find it helpful to include a section on assumptions at the beginning of your content, especially for longer, more complex materials such as training manuals: that section would explain to the reader who the document has been designed for and what assumptions have been made, such as familiarity with a particular software application or business sector.

ASSUMPTIONS AND ACCESSIBILITY

Here's a crucially important assumption that you shouldn't make. It's the assumption that everybody who's accessing your content has the same physical abilities that you do. That isn't always the case.

Many people use assistive technologies such as screen readers to access content. Others can't use mice or touchscreens and rely on keyboard controls. This is particularly important if you're creating digital media, as it may require you to think about how you present links or use images.

The Web Accessibility Initiative has an excellent guide to accessibility – including guidelines that the UK Government has made mandatory for its own sites – at www.w3.org/WAI/users/.

Accessibility of a different kind is relevant here too. Technical writing that's published online isn't necessarily going to be viewed on a desktop or laptop PC. It might be on a tablet, or a smartphone or even a smartwatch. If so, that requires a serious rethink of how you present your information: usability guru Jakob Neilsen recommends half the word count you'd have in print and a limit of one idea per paragraph.[14]

The UK Government has produced extensive guidance on accessibility for digital services, and that guidance also includes links to resources for testing content. You'll find the most up-to-date version at www.gov.uk/service-manual/technology/testing-for-accessibility.

With technical writing it's a very good idea to consider not just the medium you're writing for today, but the other mediums your writing might be published in, in the future. That doesn't mean writing for every conceivable platform from print to pixels. But if you've structured your project or document in such a way that it can be repackaged quickly and easily then you might be saving yourself a lot of work in the not too distant future.

JUNK THE JARGON, BANISH BUZZWORDS AND ABOLISH ACRONYMS

Jargon and acronyms can be valuable. IT needs to talk about the IoT, SaaS, SLAs or XML. Surgeons need to communicate

---

[14] Jakob Nielsen (1 October 1997) *How users read on the web.* Nielsen Norman Group. Available from: www.nngroup.com/articles/how-users-read-on-the-web/

with their team in perfect clarity without scaring the patient. Financial services businesses need jargon to differentiate between very complex products.

Used correctly, jargon and acronyms can be very useful. They streamline communications – an A&E doctor can ask for the patient's BP and the nurse or paramedic hears 'blood pressure' and provides the systolic and diastolic blood pressure readings the doctor needs to know. 'BP' saves everybody a lot of time.

The problems occur when the other person doesn't know what you mean. If you're using terms or acronyms the reader doesn't understand, you might as well make up your own words and tell them to fimble the jingjang until the squeeble meebles for all the good it'll do.

The armed forces have a particularly large collection of fimbles, jingjangs, squeebles and meebles: the Ministry of Defence's list of acronyms used in the armed forces for job titles, specific places and tools is nearly 400 pages long. Those acronyms are no doubt valuable in the theatre of war or in effective military communications. However, they're meaningless to those of us who never need to refer to 2SL/CNH (the Second Sea Lord Commander in Chief Naval Home Command).

In technical writing, don't use jargon or acronyms unless you're absolutely certain that your audience will immediately understand them. Even then, consider whether you need to use them at all. If they are the most effective way to communicate your message, that's great – but always explain them in full the first time you use them; don't just say 'TLA' without explaining that it's short for three-letter acronym.

If jargon or acronyms are making your text harder to follow, write in plain English instead.

That brings us to business buzzwords, which are often the very opposite of plain English. Buzzwords are in the air when a tech chief executive officer (CEO) – or more likely, a 'Thought Leader' – talks about surfacing content when they mean showing people stuff; when somebody says they'll ping you when they mean they'll send you an email or call you; when somebody doesn't have the bandwidth to say they're too busy. All too often business buzzwords replace perfectly good words with lesser, more vague, more pretentious alternatives.

KEY TAKEAWAYS

- Don't assume your readers' level of knowledge and experience.
- Never assume your readers have the same physical abilities you do.
- Acronyms and jargon are only useful if everybody understands them.

6   VANQUISH VAGUENESS

Vagueness is the enemy of effective business writing and technical writing in particular. Unfortunately, it's a very clever foe and tends to sneak in if you're not keeping an eye out for it.

BE PRECISE

Time is particularly fertile ground for vagueness, because we're often vague about time in normal conversation. Unfortunately, while terms such as 'back in a tick', 'there in a jiffy', 'I'll be with you shortly' help to keep English colourful, they're not much help when you're trying to communicate something specific. Watch out for such terms creeping into your writing and replace them with actual times or periods of time: if something should take less than 10 minutes say so, because that means if it's still churning away after 30 minutes the reader will know something is wrong.

Similarly, don't use terms such as 'overnight' if you have a minimum number of hours in mind. In such cases you can still say 'overnight', but you should qualify it by adding 'or for at least X hours'.

Sometimes we don't even include a time. 'All systems should be backed up weekly' is perfectly good advice, but if it's supposed to happen on the dot at 12 midnight every Tuesday then say so.

And did you spot the 'should'? That's a no-no too.

DON'T LEAVE WIGGLE ROOM

The word 'should' is a pet hate for many writers because it gives the reader wiggle room. It sounds strong but it's actually weak: if you write that the system should be fully reset every 12 hours, you're effectively telling the reader that you'd like them to do that, but it's okay if they forget or have other priorities. It's much weaker than 'must', which is the word you should usually use instead.

I used 'should' there instead of 'must' because I'm offering advice, not telling you what to do. If you're doing the latter, don't use 'should', or other words with wiggle room.

BE SPECIFIC

As with time, when you're describing quantities it's usually better to use specific, measurable units rather than vague terms such as 'a handful', 'a few' or 'several'. You may need to be specific about temperatures for an industrial process, quantities for a chemical reaction or the expected mean time between failures on hard disks. And if you're trying to get the board to green-light a project, you'll need to be very specific about any financial figures or calculations.

While it's important to be specific, make sure you aren't being too specific. If you're writing documentation that covers multiple products, plants or processes it needs to be accurate for all of those products, plants or processes. If a particular measurement, command or control only applies to one or some items, places or systems within a larger grouping then you'll need to provide the correct data, quantities or instructions for the others.

KEY TAKEAWAYS

- Avoid vague terms such as 'a while' or 'not too long'.
- Use measurable quantities wherever possible or appropriate.
- Don't use terms that leave wiggle room.

7   DON'T BE YOURSELF

Personality is a wonderful thing in writing. Unless it's in technical writing.

Technical writing needn't be dry or dull. I'm all in favour of writing that's as interesting and as accessible as it can possibly be. However, personality can be a problem because it can sometimes get in the way of what you're trying to achieve.

THE IMPORTANCE OF CLARITY

Effective communication is all about getting your message across as clearly as possible, and sometimes personality prevents you from doing that. Some of the things that make us so interesting and popular in our everyday lives aren't quite as lovable on paper. Jokes may fall flat, comparisons may confuse and what we think makes a piece more entertaining may just annoy.

Humour is a good example. Humour is a very subjective thing: for example, I like the dry, self-aware comedy of Stewart Lee and the bile of Frankie Boyle; others prefer the much gentler observational humour of Michael McIntyre or Sarah Millican. And somebody somewhere is clearly enjoying *Mrs Brown's Boys* and voting for it in every awards ceremony.

Those differences are part of life's rich tapestry, but they can become chasms in technical writing. A joke I'll find gut-bustingly funny may well baffle everybody but me, or it may rely on shared cultural references that simply don't translate to other areas, countries or cultures. That means it becomes wasted words: it doesn't help to communicate an idea and might even sabotage that communication.

It's not just humour. Slang is often limited to very specific geographical areas, so a term that everybody in Gateshead uses may be completely alien to Glaswegians. Comparisons to things only work if the readers know what the things are in the first place, as discussed in the example of young people and 'Save' icons in Chapter 5. There are generation gaps as well as national and cultural ones.

Effective technical writing means speaking the right language. Speaking the **right** language doesn't necessarily mean speaking the **same** language. A 40-something manager attempting to write in the language his or her teenage employees might use socially is heading into embarrassing-parent territory, and such attempts can seem patronising even when you get the language right. However, the wider your audience, the more welcoming your language needs to be.

Speaking the right language means using language that is clear, appropriate and gets your message across without any confusion or anybody having to Google the terms you use.

KEY TAKEAWAYS

- Effective writing means speaking the right language for your audience.

- Humour and geographical or cultural references are best avoided in technical writing.

- Your reader should never have to Google to understand your writing.

8 STICK TO THE STORY

Technical writing is all about getting the most from the least: nobody wants to wade through something the size of a brick just to find out what button to press or what headgear they need to order. Always keep in mind the who, what and how we explored earlier: who am I writing for, what information do they need and how do they need to receive it?

It's very important to keep putting yourself in the readers' shoes. For example, I love wordplay, puns and bad jokes and tend to use them in headlines. And when I do, editors come along and take them all out again because they aren't helping the reader.

Think of the frustration when your car has a flat tyre and you're trying to find the tyre pressures and you're already late for a meeting and the handbook doesn't have a great big headline saying TYRE PRESSURES ARE ON THIS PAGE and eventually you find the information but it's in pounds per square inch and the inflator at the garage shows the pressure in bars. It's not a time when you want to see a joke about being 'so tyred' in the handbook.

It's exactly the same when you're writing for others. The document you're working on may be something the end user refers to when they're having a really bad day, the boss is breathing down their neck, customers are being unreasonable and they can't remember exactly what the procedure is. Give them the information they need as quickly as possible; in some cases, such as press releases and technical reports, that might mean putting the crucial information in the very first sentence.

Any obstacle between the reader and the information they need is going to make their day worse.

Here are seven obstacles to watch out for.

1. LONG PARAGRAPHS

I'm not suggesting that your paragraphs should consist of a sentence.

Or even a few words.

But sometimes that's a really good way of emphasising something important.

Once again, moderation is key. If you write everything in really short, punchy sentences you can end up going too far: it's hard to read and feels a bit like somebody's shouting at you through a megaphone. But equally, sentences and paragraphs that go on for days aren't easy to read either.

2. DENSE BLOCKS OF TEXT

Avoid dense blocks of text. Break them up with headings and sub-headings, which make the text look more welcoming. They can also be navigational aids for the reader, and in electronic media that means they can be linked directly so the reader can get straight to the content they need.

Bulleted and numbered lists can be helpful too. They break up the page and once again direct the readers' eyes to key information.

3. IRRELEVANT OR USELESS GRAPHICS

I'll sing the praises of appropriate images throughout this book. However, if you've ever sighed at a PowerPoint slide consisting solely of a clipart man with a giant question mark over his head, you'll know that images don't necessarily add value.

Images need to justify their existence in your documents. What value do they add? Do they make the concept clearer? Do they present a piece of information in the most useful and accessible way? If not, revise them or take them out altogether.

4. POOR PUNCTUATION

On the front cover of *Tails* magazine, an article for dog lovers, the heading promised something a bit more gory than the usual doggy fare: 'Rachael Ray finds inspiration in cooking her family and her dog'. A single comma would have prevented us from imagining cannibalism and pooch-poaching.

That one turned out to be fake[15] – somebody had Photoshopped out the commas from the real cover – but in 1998 *The Sunday Times* really did give its readers the mental image of Peter Ustinov meeting 'Nelson Mandela, an 800-year-old demigod and a dildo collector'.[16]

I've gone for funny examples but sometimes poor punctuation can have serious consequences: the lack of a comma was the subject of a $17 million lawsuit between a US dairy company and its delivery drivers.[17]

5. TOO MUCH INFORMATION

This is a particular hazard if you're translating information given to you by experts: sometimes they're so excited about the subject that they want everybody to know every aspect

---

[15] See https://mashable.com/2012/06/12/rachael-ray-tails-fake-magazine/

[16] Referenced in this article by Stan Carey (2011) *The Oxford, Harvard, or serial comma*. Available from https://stancarey.wordpress.com/2011/06/30/the-oxford-harvard-or-serial-comma/#more-8519

[17] See www.nytimes.com/2017/03/16/us/oxford-comma-lawsuit.html

of everything to do with it. And that's great, unless you're a harassed first line support tech who just wants to know what to do with today's furious customer, or a sales rep who needs to let the client know the tech specs of the product they're pitching. By all means explain and inform, but not if it's irrelevant to what your reader wants or needs.

Many documents are made much better by making them much shorter. Cut, cut, cut some more and then cut a bit more after that.

6. FORGETTING TO INCLUDE THE 'HOW'

This is another problem based on knowing too much. Sometimes a document will ask the reader to do something without explaining how to do it. For example, we all know what 'reboot the PC' means. Don't we?

Be vigilant for little pieces of assumed knowledge like that one. If you're certain that your intended audience already knows the 'how' then that's great. If you're not certain, explain it or link to an explanation.

7. UNCLEAR NAVIGATION AIDS

This is the missing TYRE PRESSURES ARE ON THIS PAGE bit I mentioned earlier. Headings and subheadings are navigation aids for readers, so make them as clear as possible on the page, in any contents page and in any index or links. As much as I love punning headlines and subheadings – and I've used them in this very book – they don't help the reader find information quickly, so they should be avoided in any technical writing project.

One of the most commonly used forms of navigation is the breadcrumb trail, which takes its name from the story of Hansel and Gretel. You see it a lot on websites, where it's so commonplace we rarely even notice it unless it isn't there. However, it works almost as well in print.

A breadcrumb trail looks something like this:

Owner's Manual > Quick reference > Tyres > Tyre pressures

Or this:

Home > Support > FAQs > Installation and registration > Installation problems

Or this:

Q-36 Space Modulator > Operating instructions > First steps > Assembly

As Hansel and Gretel found, breadcrumbs enable you to retrace your steps – so in the examples above, if we find that the section we're in doesn't have the precise bit of information we're looking for we can go back one step and try another option.

There's a very good chance you use a similar structure when you're putting your project together, so it should be simple to let the reader use it too.

KEY TAKEAWAYS

- Use graphics and other variations, but do so sparingly.
- Watch out for little assumptions.
- Breadcrumb navigation helps readers and writers alike.

9 BE ACTIVE: WHY YOU SHOULD AVOID THE PASSIVE VOICE AND WEAK VERBS

One of the most common – and easily avoided – traps that writers can fall into is using what's called the 'passive voice'. In technical writing, it can make reading feel rather like swimming through treacle.

The passive voice is when your writing is unnecessarily distant and stilted. The classic example is writing 'it was decided that' instead of 'we decided' or 'they decided'. It's still correct, but it's wordier and less punchy.

WHY WEAK WORDS MAKE WRITING WORSE

The passive voice relies on weak 'passive' verbs instead of punchy 'active' ones. For example, somebody using the passive voice might write:

> The big red button should be pushed by the user.

When it's much better to say:

> Push the big red button.

In the first example, it's not clear who the subject of the sentence is. Who is this mysterious user?

In the second sentence, the subject is clearly the reader, and you're telling them exactly what they should do. This approach works well in instructional writing, such as how-tos and tutorials where the intended audience will be using it as a step by step guide: by issuing direct commands – press this, click on that, call this number – it's really clear what the reader is supposed to be doing in each step.

Here's another unnecessarily wordy example:

> The tablet is powered on by the user pressing the sleep/ wake button.

It's better to say:

> To turn the tablet on, press the sleep/wake button.

The passive voice tends to be less direct. For example, instead of:

> It has been noted that some employees have been using their work PCs for personal browsing.

It'd be better to say:

> Don't use your work PC for personal browsing.

This example isn't necessarily wrong:

> The ticket can then be escalated by the technician to second line support.

But this is simpler and clearer:

> Refer the case to second line support.

You've probably seen something like this:

> Employees are not permitted to...

But this does the same job:

> You must not...

And this is even more effective:

> Don't...

The difference isn't always quite so dramatic, but effective technical writing is all about getting the maximum effect from your words. Avoiding the passive voice helps with that.

I'm not suggesting you never use the passive voice, but I recommend using the active voice whenever it's more effective. As always, the goal is to make your writing as clear and as accessible as possible.

KEY TAKEAWAYS

- Use 'we decided', not 'it was decided that'.
- Keep your language as clear as possible.

10 DIAGRAMS, LISTS AND GRAPHICS

Technical writing is all about clarity and efficiency. Sometimes the clearest, most efficient way to present information is to use fewer words in a more effective way. That might mean presenting the information as a numbered or bulleted list, or as an infographic. Or it might mean putting the information across in a flow chart.

The items I'll describe in this chapter are like salt. Used sparingly they can bring out the flavour of your writing and enhance what you've created. Use too much and they'll overwhelm it and possibly ruin it. As ever, less is more.

LISTY BUSINESS

From our childhood letters to Santa to the to-do lists pinging on our phones, we use lists for all kinds of things. There's a good reason for that: lists are very effective.

Numbered lists make it easy to see sequential information – do **this** and then **this** and then **that** and then **that** – while bulleted lists enable you to present information in a way that's a lot more attractive than standard blocks of text.

Tables can make numerical information a lot less frightening and related data easier to compare and contrast.

GO WITH THE FLOW (CHART)

Flow charts are hardly rocket science – unless, that is, they're used in rocket science. And they are. The National Aeronautics and Space Administration (NASA) used flow charts extensively in its space programme, but flow charts are just as effective in explaining complex mechanical operations like the one in Figure 10.1.

Figure 10.1 Flow chart based on the 'engineering flow chart' meme[18]

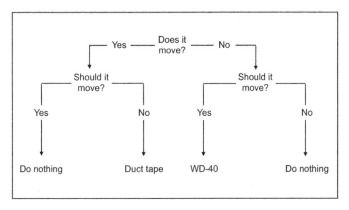

If you've worked in the chemicals industry you'll probably be familiar with process flow diagrams, which provide a bird's eye view of what's going on in the plant. If you program, you may have used flow charts to set out the structure before you start coding. If you're involved in project management, you'll be familiar with deployment flow charts and so on.

Flow charts are particularly useful when the intended reader may not have the time to read a lot of text, where you're trying to show something that's a real pain to describe (organisational

---

[18] See www.flickr.com/photos/dullhunk/7214525854. Original artist unknown.

charts are a good example of this) or where your writing is going to be in a place where normal text isn't appropriate. For example, details of how to evacuate a building and where to assemble afterwards aren't the kind of thing you'll read at a leisurely pace; you read them when the alarm's going off, everybody's panicking and you think you can smell smoke.

It's a similar story with procedures that need to be followed in stressful or time-limited circumstances, or with information that needs to be as clear as possible for the widest possible audience.

It's important to remember that a flow chart isn't necessarily a good or a bad way of presenting information. It all depends on how you use it. A flow chart that looks like spaghetti or whose boxes contain impenetrable acronyms isn't going to help anybody.

OTHER KINDS OF CHARTS

There are all kinds of charts that enable us to present information visually. The four most common types are discussed in this section.

Line charts

Cartoonists love using these ones when they draw businessmen and women. A line chart (Figure 10.2) shows numerical information as a line, and is commonly used to show trends such as profits over time, increases or decreases in production numbers, fluctuations in exchange rates or anything else that's gone up or down.

Bar charts

Simple bar charts (Figure 10.3) can be used in the same way as line charts to show changes over time: instead of a line between points, each value is shown as a horizontal or vertical bar. However, bar charts are better suited to showing different

Figure 10.2 Example line chart

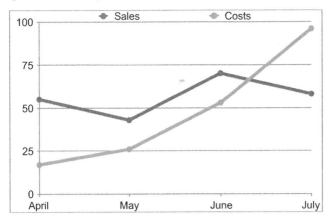

Figure 10.3 Example bar chart

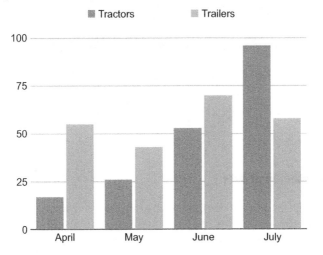

pieces of information: for example, a company might use bars to show how many customers bought product X, how many product Y and how many bought product Z.

Pie charts

The familiar circle broken into slices (Figure 10.4): each slice shows a percentage or proportion of the whole.

Figure 10.4 Example pie chart

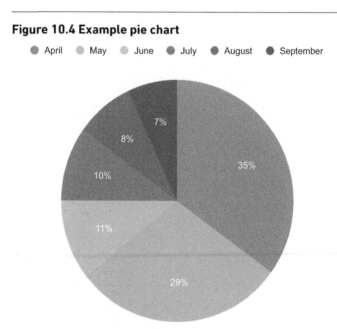

Cartesian charts

Simple charts are designed to present one kind of information: average temperatures, perhaps, or number of tractors produced. That means they usually have one set of numbers, usually on the Y-axis (the vertical line); the X-axis (which runs left to right) shows categories or periods of time. So, to take our tractor example, the X-axis would list each month and the Y-axis would show the number of tractors produced that month.

Cartesian charts have numerical values on each axis. They're used to show the relationship between two kinds of numbers, so, for example, you might have marketing spend on the X-axis and total sales on the Y, as in the example in Figure 10.5.

Figure 10.5 Example Cartesian chart

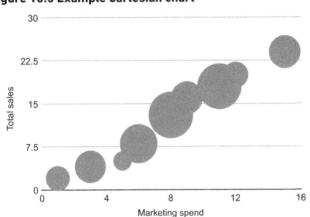

KEEP AWAY FROM THE CLIPART

Many computer programs such as Microsoft Word and its imitators enable you to add all kinds of items such as shapes, clipart, special text effects and so on. And many people believe that by doing so, Word and its imitators have made the world considerably more annoying as a result. The various tools have certainly helped people create some truly terrible documents, and, as a result, it's a good idea to steer clear of the most clichéd ones, such as overly fancy text effects and poorly drawn comic characters.

GOOD GRAPHICS

A well-chosen graphic or image with a specific purpose can enhance technical writing. There are lots of great resources for good free images on the internet, but be careful: just because something's online doesn't mean you can use it without payment. Look for sites that explicitly give you permission to use their content, such as pexels.com, which states 'the pictures are completely free to be used **for any legal purpose**'.[19] That includes commercial use.

One of the most common ways creators can give other people permission to use their content is to label images with a Creative Commons license. That enables the person who created the image to specify how it can be used, and you can search for Creative Commons images in Google Image Search. You can find the different licence types at creativecommons.org, but the ones you're looking for must **not** contain the tag 'NC' for non-commercial. If they do, it means the copyright owner doesn't want them used by businesses.

Copyright must be explicit. If you aren't absolutely certain that you have the right to use an image, you must assume that you don't have the right to use it.

KEY TAKEAWAYS

- Use lists to break up forbidding blocks of text.
- Keep away from the clipart.
- Don't assume you can use a graphic or image from the internet for free.

---

[19] Under the Creative Commons Zero (CC0) license.

Printed by Amazon POD

11 EVERYBODY NEEDS AN EDITOR

Many writers like to complain about editing. It's often tongue in cheek – for example, the novelist Ian Rankin likes to tell Twitter about the cruelty of his editors forcing him to fix things when he thought he was finished – but sometimes it's genuine. The writer has produced a masterpiece and hates being told that it isn't perfect.

The writer is usually wrong, because almost everybody benefits from having an editor look at their work.

No matter how much effort and expertise you've put into your writing, the first version can almost always be improved. There's a reason newspapers, magazines and book publishers employ editors: they take the writers' work and make it better.

Editing is particularly important in technical writing because mistakes can have consequences. A mistake in a novel about pirates isn't the end of the world. A mistake in a bomb disposal procedure manual may well be. Your writing may need to be checked for legal compliance, or to ensure that an absolute beginner can follow it.

No matter what kind of technical writing you're producing, it's a very good idea to have somebody else cast a (constructively) critical eye over it. That's easier than ever before thanks to collaborative tools such as Microsoft Word's or Google Docs' collaboration and commenting features. And if there isn't anybody who can do that, you can become your own editor.

But first...

LET GO OF YOUR EGO

There's a very good chance that the bits of writing you like best are the first things you need to get rid of. That excellent joke, snippet of a song lyric or *Game of Thrones* reference would be great in informal writing, but there's rarely a place for it in technical writing. Think of it like optimising programming code, removing duplicates from a database or compressing files. You've created a piece of writing and now you need to maximise its efficiency.

WHAT TO LOOK FOR WHEN YOU'RE EDITING

There are five key things to look for when you're editing technical writing.

- accuracy;
- simplicity;
- brevity;
- effectiveness;
- sheer unrelenting tedium.

Let's take each one in turn.

ACCURACY

If a piece of technical writing isn't accurate, it's a failure at best and downright dangerous at worst. If you're telling the reader to cut the blue wire when you mean the red one, to fill the tank with petrol when you mean diesel, or to press Cmd + X when you mean Cmd + V then you're committing the ultimate sin of technical writing: telling somebody to do the wrong thing.

Accuracy is just as crucial even when you aren't writing how-tos. If you're writing about regulations or legislation, there is usually a very specific set of criteria that somebody or their organisation must follow; and if you're using figures, even a minor error could throw the entire formula or final total horribly out of whack.

And of course, there's your spelling and grammar. If you're writing for other languages, it's a good idea to switch your writing app's automatic checkers (if it has them) to the language you're using. For example, switching to US English when you're writing for American readers will ensure you use 'center' instead of 'centre' and 'organize' instead of 'organise' and so on.

Measurements matter

Using measurements in technical writing is rather like using measurements in a recipe: there's a world of difference – and possibly a world of pain – between 1tsp and 1tbsp of Sadistic Steve's Frighteningly Fierce Painful Pepper Sauce.

Some measurements are easily confused. For example:

• Bits (b) vs bytes (B).

A gigabyte (1GB) is eight times larger than a gigabit (1Gb). This is often confused when describing connection speeds, which are usually expressed in megabits or gigabits: a 1Mbps connection will download 1 megabit per second, but it needs eight seconds to download a megabyte.

• KB, MB and GB

In IT, prefixes don't use the same system as they do in the rest of the world – so while we all understand K to mean 1,000 when we're talking about kilograms or kilometres, IT uses binary and not decimal numbering. That means in IT, K means 1,024 and not 1,000. A kilobyte is 1,024 bytes, a megabyte is 1,048,576 (1,024 × 1,024) bytes, a gigabyte is 1,073,741,824 (1,024 × 1,024 × 1,024) bytes and so on.

Don't just ensure that you use the correct units. Make sure the readers know exactly what you mean too.

Compliance

Compliance means following the rules. Those rules aren't just the rules of effective writing and of the organisation you're writing for. They may also be rules set down by external bodies. Some industries, such as financial services, the pharmaceutical industry, healthcare and the oil and gas industries, have very strict regulations that they must adhere to and those regulations may apply to the documentation you're producing or the information you're giving others.

When helpers aren't helping

Be very, very wary of computerised helpers such as AutoCorrect and AutoComplete when you're creating technical writing and keep a sharp eye out for their errors when editing. It's all too easy for the automated helper to replace something correct that it doesn't expect with something incorrect it's happy with.

It's a similar story with spellcheckers and grammar checkers, which don't always catch things such as homophones, which are words that sound the same but which are spelled differently. 'Their', 'they're' and 'there' are homophones. So are write/right, to/two and mail/male. If you're relying on a computer spelling or grammar checker, it's a good idea to get a colleague to look over your work too.

Opinions and anecdotes

Technical writing is no place for opinions and anecdotes unless they help to illuminate something that's otherwise hard to explain. It should be absolutely clear what's a fact and what isn't, and if something isn't a fact it needs to be doing an awful lot of work to justify its inclusion in your text.

SIMPLICITY

Appropriately enough, this one's simple. You're looking for anything that makes your writing less friendly to the reader:

too-long paragraphs, unnecessary use of long words, the passive voice, jargon and anything else that might make the reader go 'eh?'

In how-tos, simplicity goes hand in hand with consistency. For example, if you're going to be telling people to press particular buttons or click particular icons it's important to keep the same formatting conventions and language every time you tell the reader to do something.

Don't forget the cliché that a picture paints a thousand words. If you're writing for print, sometimes no amount of excellent writing will be as effective as a picture with a big red arrow on it. Online, a YouTube video may do a better job than 10 pages of perfect prose.

BREVITY

It's very easy to write too much – I do it all the time, because I find it's easier to write too much and then make it more punchy when I edit – and some forms of flab are easy to spot and take out. For example, irrelevant background information should be the first thing to go.

When you're editing a piece of technical writing, the constant question should be: 'does this bit help the reader?' 'Would this section be just as clear, just as helpful, if I took this bit out?' If the answer is yes, take it out. You'll be surprised by how much you can remove: you can typically reduce your total word count by around 20 per cent while making your document more readable and more useful.

EFFECTIVENESS

Technical writing exists to do a specific job. There's no room for vagueness: your writing is either an effective manual, procedure, tutorial or guidance note, or it isn't.

One of the best ways to evaluate technical writing is to get somebody else to review it or, if appropriate, test it. Ideally that somebody should be much less knowledgeable about or experienced in the thing you're writing about than you are, because most of the time that's the kind of person you're writing for. If you're writing about something highly technical, it's also a good idea to have an expert check it for accuracy.

Let's say your writing is a how-to for a new software application that nobody in the company (other than you, of course) knows how to use. The test of its effectiveness is clearly whether somebody who isn't you can get the results they want without getting lost, confused or terrified. And it's crucial that if they do get lost, confused or terrified that they provide feedback to tell you what the problem is and where they encountered it. You can't fix problems you don't know about.

Real-world testing is a particularly good way to spot the kind of assumptions we all make when we know a subject inside out: what's really obvious to us might not be obvious to somebody else, and feedback enables us to fill in any gaps that might cause confusion.

Think of it like driving a car. So many of the things you do when driving are completely automatic. You don't need to remember which pedal to press when you want to brake, or what you need to do to change gear, or where the windscreen wipers are. But when you sat in a car for the first time, you didn't know any of those things. The same applies to someone who's just joined the department, or who hasn't encountered a particular system or policy before.

Testing and getting feedback helps you to identify any bits that need more detail.

There are all kinds of ways to get feedback. For small projects or small groups, it might be as simple as having a conversation with the person after they've used your document, or watching someone trying to achieve their objective with your document. For big projects and groups, you might use analytics software to track page read times, links clicked and other important information, or you might have a feedback link on online documentation. You might use surveys, or group meetings.

When you're testing your writing, it's worth returning to the personas we explored earlier. The feedback method that suits you best might be the least appropriate for your target personas, and there's a world of difference between assessing documentation in a classroom environment and in a real working environment with all its stresses and strains. The more you tailor things to the people who will be using your content, the more useful the feedback you'll get.

SHEER TEDIUM

Technical writing is often boring to read. Sometimes that's unavoidable because you're writing about something that's boring. But sometimes it's because you've produced something unnecessarily boring by accident.

One of the best ways to check for boring content is to read your writing aloud. Sentences that looked just fine on paper may have you propping open your eyeballs by the mid-point. Overly long descriptions can have you losing the will to live long before the end of the paragraph.

I'm not suggesting that you should write in the style of an overly caffeinated children's presenter, and, as explained in previous chapters, humour in particular doesn't translate or age very well. But if your writing is an alphabet soup of acronyms and you rarely use a sentence when 16 paragraphs will do, there's a good chance you could make it a lot more reader-friendly. Can it be explained in a more interesting way, or with an even better example? Could the language be simplified?

Mix it up

One way to keep your writing interesting is to vary the length of sentences. On average, a good sentence is around 15 to 25 words long, but if you wrote everything to a 25-word target you'd end up with something that felt really weird and robotic.

The sentences in that last paragraph were 14 words and 32 words respectively. And sometimes shorter is better (that one's five words).

When you're writing, take a look at it in full-page view. Is any paragraph a forbidding rectangular block of 87 words with precious little white space and sentences that go on forever, adding lots of words to the original point without actually doing anything constructive, resulting in something that if you were to read out in one breath would have you keeling over because it takes so long to read that you'd run out of oxygen long before you reached the second-last comma, which came before another bunch of words that did absolutely nothing of any use whatsoever?

You get the point, I'm sure.

You can mix things up in other ways too. A well-chosen image or embedded YouTube video can often help illuminate a tricky subject, while good use of typography and formatting, such as breaking long sections into headed sub-sections, can help draw the reader's eye to the most important bits of information. If you're writing for an internet or intranet system, you can hyperlink to related or background information instead of including it, or provide fast links to related parts of your own content. Just remember to keep checking links to ensure they're still current. Nothing dents confidence in an online system more than a 404: Page Not Found error.

KEY TAKEAWAYS

- Everyone benefits from editing.
- Test and get feedback from others wherever possible.
- Always ask: 'is this the best way to get the message across?'

12 THE TECHNICAL WRITING HOUSE OF HORRORS

One of my favourite examples of a technical writing disaster is fictional, but very funny: in the fake rock documentary *This Is Spinal Tap*, the guitarist's plans for a Stonehenge stage set are written perfectly, but he uses quotation marks (for inches) instead of the single apostrophe for the measurements in feet that he actually meant. Cue cowled figures dancing around what looks like a tiny garden ornament.

Unfortunately, real-world examples aren't quite so entertaining, as the 'million-dollar comma' case (see the next section) demonstrates. I'm presenting these as confidence boosters: everybody makes mistakes – that's why reviewing and editing is so important – but I bet you won't make mistakes as devastating as these.

WHEN COMMAS COST

The million-dollar comma case hinged on a single punctuation mark. Canadian telecoms firm Bell Aliant had a five-year deal with cable TV firm Rogers Communications to let the latter use its telegraph poles, but it cancelled the contract after a year. Rogers claimed that the cancellation was illegal and would cost it 1 million Canadian dollars; Bell Aliant argued that the position of a comma in one clause of the 14-page contract clearly meant it could cancel the deal after one year and not five.

This was the sentence in question.[20]

---

[20] See www.nytimes.com/2006/10/25/business/worldbusiness/25comma.html

> This agreement shall be effective from the date it is made and shall continue in force for a period of five (5) years from the date it is made, and thereafter for successive five (5) year terms, unless and until terminated by one year prior notice in writing by either party.

The argument was over that second comma before 'unless and until terminated'. The sentence was intended to say that the contract would be in place for five years, and after that the contract could be terminated with one year's notice. But Bell Aliant argued that the comma clearly meant that the contract could be terminated with one year's notice at any time, not just after five years.

Rogers eventually won the case, but it was a hollow victory. The Canadian Radio-Television and Telecommunications Commission said that while Rogers was the injured party the Commission had no jurisdiction over power poles, so it couldn't do anything about the money Rogers claimed to have lost.

More recently, the case of *O'Connor v. Oakhurst Dairy* in Maine, USA in 2017 hinged on another single comma.[21] By law, firms in Maine have to pay overtime to anybody that works more than 40 hours per week. However, there's an exception in the case of perishable products that have to be processed while they're still fresh. The law says that means no overtime for 'the canning, processing, preserving, freezing, drying, marketing, storing, packing for shipment or distribution' of meat, fish and other perishable products.

The case hinged on 'packing for shipment or distribution'. The drivers said that it clearly meant packing for distribution, not the actual distribution, so therefore the drivers should be paid overtime. The dairy said that the law clearly listed 'packing for shipment' separately from 'distribution', so therefore the drivers shouldn't be paid overtime.

---

[21] See www.newyorker.com/culture/culture-desk/a-few-words-about-that-ten-million-dollar-serial-comma

After a lot of time and a lot of legal fees, a US court of appeals found in the drivers' favour. They haven't won at the time of writing, but they're free to take their case to another court. If they win, the dairy will have to cough up a whopping $10 million in wages.

What these examples demonstrate is that punctuation isn't trivial. Had the legal advice in the Maine dairy case finished with 'packing for shipment, or distribution' then the writer might not have cost the dairy $10 million.

THE CONVERSION THAT COST A SPACESHIP

In 1998, NASA's Climate Orbiter spacecraft was lost in space after going too close to Mars. It turned out that different teams within NASA were using different measurements, with one team using metric measurements and the other imperial; the result was the loss of a craft worth $125 million and the data it was sent to gather.[22]

THE 'S' THAT KILLED A COMPANY

In 2009, a firm called Taylor & Son Ltd went into administration in England. Unfortunately, it was entered into the Companies House database as Taylor & Sons Ltd, a completely different firm. Within three weeks the 124-year-old Taylor & Sons was forced into bankruptcy as 3,000 suppliers cancelled their contracts with what they believed to be a company about to be liquidated. The typo cost Companies House millions in legal bills, but that was little comfort to the 250 people who lost their jobs.[23]

---

[22] See https://en.wikipedia.org/wiki/Mars_Climate_Orbiter
[23] See www.theguardian.com/law/shortcuts/2015/jan/28/typo-how-one-mistake-killed-a-family-business-taylor-and-sons

WHEN XXX COSTS $$$

The now-defunct Banner Travel Services, a California travel agent, sued *Yellow Pages* for $18 million after it was wrongly listed as a specialist in 'erotic' destinations: the listing should have said 'exotic'. Banner claimed the typo lost it 80 per cent of its regular customers.[24]

THE £52 MILLION COMMA

If you thought the million-dollar comma was bad, in 1999 aerospace giant Lockheed Martin lost a whopping $70 million (around £52 million) because it put a comma in the wrong place in a formula – an error of just one decimal point – in a sales contract.[25]

---

[24] See www.rd.com/culture/expensive-typos/
[25] See http://money.cnn.com/1999/06/18/worldbiz/lockheed/

AFTERWORD

Have you ever made pasta from a recipe? If you have, you've probably encountered a great example of poor technical writing.

Many recipes will tell you to cook your pasta in salted water. But very few of those recipes tell you how much salt should be in that water. And that's crucial information because if your water isn't salty enough, your pasta won't have that authentic flavour. The oft-quoted 'as salty as the sea!' explanation isn't helpful either unless you happen to have some sea water handy for comparison.

How much salt should we use?

Good technical writing would give the harassed cook the fastest answer – a teaspoon and a half per litre – and provide more detailed information for cooking geeks like me who have more than one kind of salt in their kitchen cupboards.

We only tend to notice technical writing when it's done badly, or when it doesn't give us what we want. Good technical writing is largely invisible. But in business, it's invaluable.

Whatever industry you're in or project you're working on, technical writing is about making somebody's life easier. That somebody may be trying to learn a new application, or follow a complex procedure. They might be selling a product, or trying to assemble one they've bought. Whatever it is, our job is to give them the information they need, when they need it, in the way that's most useful to them. And when we do, we make the world a better place.

Happy writing.

INDEX